# ideals
## FRIENDSHIP

Friendship is a ballad,
A melody never forgotten,
Satisfying the senses,
Its beauty remaining
In the chambers of the mind.

Friendship is the warm feeling
Of candlelight,
Memories of years shared,
Flickering like shadows
Against the wall of life.

Friendship is gold,
Bright and shiny,
A treasure to be held
Gently in the palm of the hand
And tucked warmly into
The corner of the heart.

Friendship is a prize
Life awards for being a friend,
That very special someone
In harmony with
All the seasons of life:
Springtime hopes and dreams,
Summer wishes and promises,
Autumn regrets
And winter's serenity.

Grace W. McKinney

**Publisher,** James A. Kuse
**Managing Editor,** Ralph Luedtke
**Editor/Ideals,** Colleen Callahan Gonring
**Associate Editor,** Linda Robinson
**Production Manager,** Mark Brunner
**Photographic Editor,** Gerald Koser
**Copy Editor,** Barbara Nevid
**Art Editor,** Duane Weaver

ISBN 0-8249-1003-6  350

IDEALS—Vol. 38, No. 4 June MCMLXXXI. IDEALS (ISSN 0019-137X) is published eight times a year,
January, February, April, June, July, September, October, November
by IDEALS PUBLISHING CORPORATION, 11315 Watertown Plank Road, Milwaukee, Wis. 53226
Second class postage paid at Milwaukee, Wisconsin. Copyright © MCMLXXXI by IDEALS PUBLISHING CORPORATION.
Postmaster, please send form 3579 to Ideals Publishing Corporation, Post Office Box 2100, Milwaukee, Wis. 53201
All rights reserved. Title IDEALS registered U.S. Patent Office.
Published simultaneously in Canada.

ONE-YEAR SUBSCRIPTION—eight consecutive issues as published—$15.95
TWO-YEAR SUBSCRIPTION—sixteen consecutive issues as published—$27.95
SINGLE ISSUES—$3.50

# Fulfillment

Martha Hood

A flower unfolds in the glowing sun,
 Opening petals one by one,
Exposing its heart to a breathless world,
 Awed by the beauty there unfurled,
Giving its fragrance o'er and o'er;
 For that's what a flower is created for.

A friend comes in with a smiling face,
 With loving eyes and gentle grace,
Showing a heart that is fond and true;
 And shadows and gloom depart from you.
Instead come beauty and joys galore,
 For that's what friends were created for.

To add to life's beauty as flowers do,
 To manifest friendships firm and true,
To serve and give, ah, that is the core
 Of what we all were created for.

# North Woods Notebook

## Benny Goodman, Ping Pong, and Fish Soup

*My husband, Bob, was the youngest of ten children born to Comb and Anna Andersen Bourgeois. The family lived in Park Falls, Wisconsin, when Bob was born on August 20, 1923; during his childhood there were several moves to farms and small towns throughout northern Wisconsin.*

*Bob's memories of his childhood remained vivid. When he talks about those distant days, the memories come alive; they are echoes of a way of life that has all but disappeared from the American scene.*

Bea Bourgeois

Following my freshman year in high school, in 1938, our family moved from Park Falls to Cornucopia, a little town on the shore of Lake Superior. The population was 691 people; it had a general store, a cheese factory, and a small fishing industry. There's still a sign on the Post Office that identifies Cornucopia as "Wisconsin's Northernmost Village."

My best friends were Honse Ehlers (his real name was Harold, but almost everyone called him Honse) and Chuck Jones. We all lived in town, and we were inseparable buddies. Our high school group also included Leo Korpas, Don Martinson, and Herbie Lawin, who lived on farms outside of the "city limits."

There was a ping pong table in Honse's basement, and if we weren't batting the ball back and forth we'd listen to his record collection—the Dorsey Brothers, Harry James, and Glen Gray and His Casa Loma Band. We knew every song Benny Goodman recorded, and we'd sing along with Helen O'Connell and The Modernaires.

Sometimes, on Sunday afternoons when the weather was nice, we'd walk along the beach, build a fire and sit on a log and talk. I think we knew war was coming, and we were scared; there wasn't much talk of going on to college, because we knew we'd all end up in the service sooner or later. These serious conversations always ended a little before two o'clock in the afternoon, because that's when the Sammy Kaye Program started and we had to get to a radio.

In the winter we ice skated on Lake Superior. We'd take a couple of old brooms and shove the snow aside to clear enough ice for skating. We loved to roller skate, too, but we had to go to Ashland, Bayfield, or Herbster to do that, because Cornie didn't have a skating rink. Chuck was an excellent skater, and we used to tease him about showing off for those "out-of-town" girls.

Very often our entertainment depended on the generosity of Albert and Herman Lawin, Herbie's brothers, because they were old enough to drive. We used to beg them to take us to Ashland to go skating or see a movie. I remember vividly that my favorite movie was King's Row; I thought the story was marvelous, and I thought Ann Sheridan was the most beautiful woman in the world.

Kids used to have pen pals in those days, and for a couple of years I kept up a steady correspondence with a boy named Jacques who lived in France and wrote to me until the war started. Once I found a girl's name under the cover on a basket of concord grapes—she was Ruth Ort in Nauvoo, Illinois. We became pen pals, and I looked forward to those letters. I wonder whatever happened to Jacques—and to Ruth Ort down in Illinois!

Honse and Chuck and I were always looking for ways to earn money. Honse's family owned a general store, so he got paid for sweeping the floors and dusting the shelves; Ehler's Store is still there on Cornucopia's main street. Chuck and I had to scrounge for paying jobs. I think at one time or another, I probably painted every house in Cornie. For awhile I worked on a mink ranch outside of town; I ground horsemeat for their food, cleaned the cages, and fed the mink. They may have gorgeous fur, but they're one of the meanest little animals there is. And, oh, do they stink!

While I was in high school I worked with the National Youth Administration. I knew how to type, so I earned about $6.50 a month typing tests for grade school students. I had a regular fan club of little kids following me around—after all, I knew what questions would be on their examinations.

Honse and Chuck and I never caused a lot of mischief in town, but every now and then we'd decide to do something foolish. One night we climbed up into the bell tower of the Russian Orthodox Church in Cornie and rang the bell, just for the heck of it. We knew we weren't supposed to do that, because when the bell rang it meant the priest had come to town—he only visited three or four times a year, so I guess we got everybody pretty excited.

Fishing was our favorite sport in the summer; we'd throw our lines into one of the local trout streams, or we'd fish on Siskiwit Lake. We'd take along some raw vegetables and a big pot one of our mothers would loan us, and as soon as we caught trout or bluegill or crappies we'd clean them, get some water in the pot, and boil up a concoction we called "fish soup." We all smacked our lips and said what good cooks we were; but to tell the truth, I never liked the stuff.

In the summer of 1940 or 1941, there was a terrible flood at Bayfield. The river had overflowed into town after several days of tremendous rains. Honse, Chuck and I went over to help; we loaded sandbags and did what we could to clean up the awful mess. Stores had been destroyed, and the water even churned through the cemetery and uprooted caskets and broke them open. It was a grotesque sight, one I've never forgotten. The drinking water had been contaminated, so we had to drink Pepsi Cola all the while we were in Bayfield. To this day, I can't stand the taste of Pepsi Cola.

After our graduation from high school in 1941, we knew that joining the armed forces was only a matter of time. Chuck enlisted in the Navy, the first one of our group to leave home. I can still remember the sadness we felt, and how difficult it was for Honse and me to leave Cornie and our families when we were drafted into the Army in 1943. We knew that some of our group wouldn't be coming back, and some didn't. Leo Korpas was killed in France on D-Day.

I was stationed in India in 1945; I was twenty-two years old and pitifully homesick. I used to write to all the guys from Cornie, and their letters to me were a tremendous boost to my morale. I was half a world away from home, in a completely foreign culture and a climate that was nearly intolerable. The temperature in India was always over 100 degrees; and it always was humid, so humid, in fact, that our uniforms and boots would mildew overnight.

A lot of movie stars came over to the China-Burma-India Theater to entertain the servicemen; for a few wonderful hours, as we watched them sing and dance, we forgot how miserable we were. I was thrilled the day it was announced that Ann Sheridan—my secret passion from the days of King's Row—would be coming with a troupe to entertain us.

The thought of seeing Ann Sheridan in person kept me going for weeks. Well, she arrived, all right. But after two days in India, she announced that she couldn't possibly tolerate the heat and humidity, and so she went flying back home.

Funny. I never felt the same about Ann Sheridan after that.

Bea Bourgeois

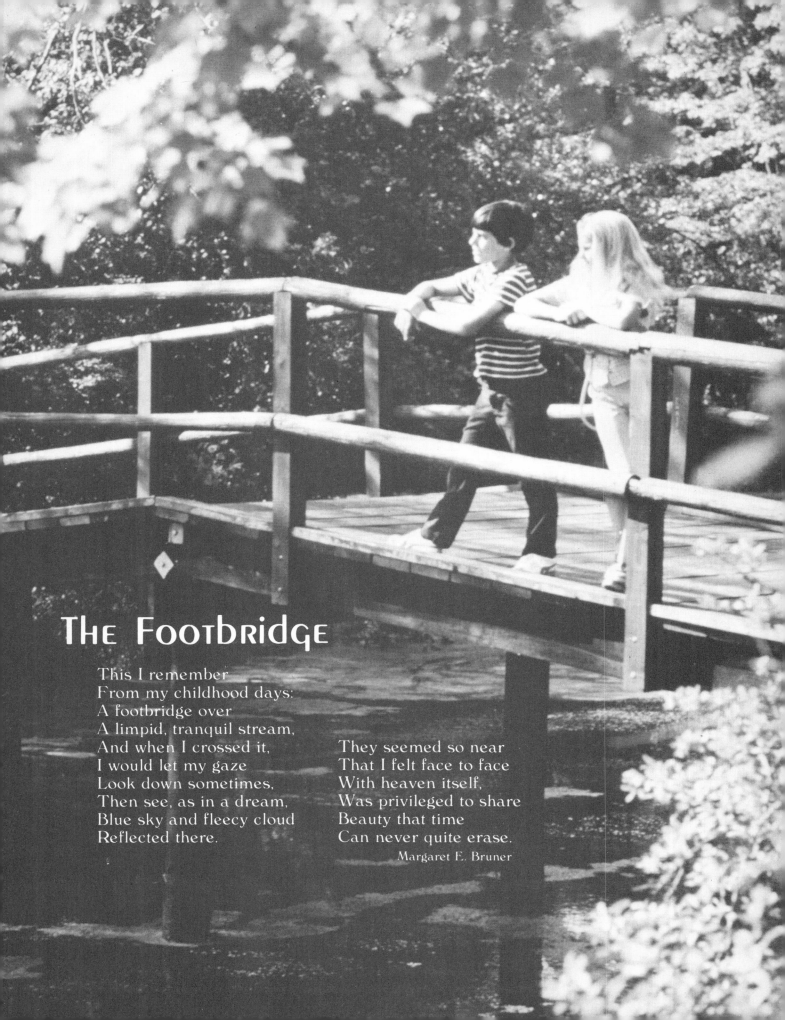

# The Footbridge

This I remember
From my childhood days:
A footbridge over
A limpid, tranquil stream,
And when I crossed it,
I would let my gaze
Look down sometimes,
Then see, as in a dream,
Blue sky and fleecy cloud
Reflected there.

They seemed so near
That I felt face to face
With heaven itself,
Was privileged to share
Beauty that time
Can never quite erase.

Margaret E. Bruner

## *Friendship Plants*

# ... To Be Nurtured Carefully

Friends are the jewels in the sands of time, the joy in a world of sadness. Friendship should be nurtured as carefully as a delicate garden plant that it may blossom forth to benefit all who share in it.

On two occasions plants were used as a means of expressing friendship between the United States and a foreign country. In each case the plant became known as the "Friendship Plant." In early 1900, *Crassula arborescens* was brought to this country from southwest Africa as a gesture of friendship, but in more recent times its common name has become jade plant. In 1952 the Central American plant, *Pilea involucrata,* was given the name Panamiga to promote friendship between the American countries. It soon became known as the South America Friendship Plant, and the name Friendship Plant has remained. Both plants are considered hardy, attractive house plants.

The jade plant, *Crassula arborescens,* can best be described as a sturdy miniature evergreen tree with fleshy oval leaves and a pleasant brown trunk and branches. There are two varieties, the small-leaf type and the more popular large-leaf variety. In a few years these plants can reach a height of three feet and an equal width. Judicial pruning can develop them into superb, symmetrical, full-bodied specimens. Some gardeners shape them to become part of miniature Japanese bonsai gardens, taking advantage of their distinctive tree-like form and oriental appearance.

Jade plants are sturdy, tolerant house plants which readily endure the house and office environments and require little care. They thrive best in a well-lighted, airy location, preferably away from the direct summer sunlight. They thrive in temperatures from 55° to 65°F, but plants readily tolerate average room temperatures. Their one great need is a well-drained soil, preferably consisting of potting soil mixed with an equal part of vermiculite or coarse sand. Poor drainage or over-watering will quickly ruin the plant. The soil should be watered only when its surface is dry. If there is no drainage hole in the pot, the bottom should be filled with pebbles or vermiculite to keep the roots from standing in wet soil. The leaves will shrivel from over or under watering.

The plants require a rest period of two or three months, usually in the fall or early winter. The rest period can be determined by the cessation of the tip growth. During this time, the soil should be kept only mildly moist, and the plants should not be fed or disturbed in any way. If the plants are over four years of age, they occasionally develop attractive, sweetly scented, light pink or white flower clusters. Following a blooming period, they will need the rest period.

New jade plants are easily developed from seed or by rooting leaves or stem cuttings. Insert the plant part in damp sand or vermiculite, and when the roots have developed, place in a small pot containing porous soil.

*Pilea involucrata,* the Panamiga, is another good house plant that is both easily grown and very tolerant of the house or office conditions. It is an attractive, erect, bushy plant, six to eight inches tall, with two-inch long, oval, deeply quilted, velvet leaves, coppery red-brown above and reddish below. The inconspicuous blooms consist of clusters of tiny green flowers extending from the ends of the stems.

Some varieties of *Pilea involucrata* include: the silver panamiga, eight to ten inches tall with two- to three-inch long scalloped leaves which are bluish silver accented with three, dark gray veins; the black-leaved panamiga, four to eight inches tall, with one and a half-inch, copper-colored leaves with purplish undersides; and the silver-tree panamiga with two- to three-inch, bronze-green leaves that have wide, silver central stripes and silver dots on the bronzy areas.

This Friendship Plant tolerates bright to low light and the normal room temperatures and humidity. Porous soil, that contains higher than average organic material, is advisable. Care must be taken to keep the soil just moderately moist, not saturated. Use pots with drainage holes. This delicate-appearing foliage plant will thrive in many nooks and crannies, including the terrarium garden. Propagate with root or stem cuttings, especially in early spring.

The two Friendship Plants have qualities that make them very successful house plants and that express the meaning of friendship. They are pleasing, tolerant and enduring, adding quality to the world around them.

Harold W. Rock

# The Light in Children's Eyes

The light that shines out every day
From children's eyes is sweet and gay,
So innocent of worldly things.
May we live so that each year brings
A deeper trust and faith to guide
Our children growing side by side.
This light can still be pure, serene,
No matter what life's tests may mean,
When families draw close to share
Unfailing love and tender care.

Louise Darcy

# God's Greatest Gift

If children play within your door
And they are all your own,
You have a radiant, shining thing,
The greatest hearts have known.

They show that God has blessed your home;
He's given of His love
And sent fulfillment of your dreams;
He smiles down from above.

He's given things which are worthwhile,
To make your life more bright.
Be worthy of His trust in you
And thank Him, day and night.

A little child within a home,
Be that home large or small,
Is evidence of God's great love,
The greatest gift of all!

Roy Z. Kemp

# June

Up to my heart in June again,
Daft and drenched in its tune again,
Over my head in the warm gold mist
On valley and hill that June has kissed!
In the sky is a lark with the sun in his throat;
Bees drone in grasses, sleepy, remote.
I remember all good, as June keeps giving
So much of music and beauty and living;
I lie on a bank by the bladed clod,
My ear to the heart of earth and God.

Elizabeth Burningham

Sunny skies of matchless blue
With fleecy clouds that glide,
Flowers fair of every hue
Abound on every side.

Showers of melody out in the field,
A meadowlark passing by,
Dipping to taste of the grasses' yield,
Then soaring into the sky.

Butterflies flit from lily to rose,
Hummingbirds drink at each bloom,
Bees hum from dawn till evening's close
In gardens of heady perfume.

Inez Briggs

# Treasure

R. Armistead Grady

Of worldly riches I have none,
And, yet, vast treasure I have won.
For children count me as their friend,
A shattered faith I've helped to mend.
A little child I've taught to laugh;
Youth holds my hand along Life's path.
And all of this has come to me,
In trade for just some love, you see.

Children dreaming—ah, lovely dreams!
All fairyland is theirs, it seems.
And you and I are cast in parts
Of king or prince, for in their hearts,
Which is their fairyland, you see,
They've made a place for you and me.
And reigning there do we not hold
A treasure greater than pure gold?

# Elusive Butterfly

Edna Moore Schultz

Please, pretty butterfly, tell your vocation.
Why do you fly to this rustic location?

Do you have friends who must travel together?
Are you intrigued with our changeable weather?

Please, busy butterfly, let me discover
Why o'er the gold and white daisy you hover.

Tell of the mystic delights that you savor.
Can you describe the delectable flavor?

Please, restless butterfly, tell me your mission.
Where will you go for your further provision?

Give me a hint of your beautiful grooming,
Always as chic as the bumblebees zooming.

Dear little butterfly, noiselessly flitting,
You're my bright moment today when you're sitting!

# Cozy Dwelling

Thelma L. Moon

It's just a room, a simple room,
With no pretentious air,
But there's a warmth that radiates
From every friendly chair.

A patterned rug adorns the floor,
The furniture is old,
And sunset clings at close of day
To paint them all with gold.

In summer, through the open door,
Warm breezes dance and play
And bring with them the fragrance of
The roses by the way.

When all the earth is wrapped in snow,
And winter's sharp winds call,
Our fireplace sends forth a glow
That dances on the wall.

It's just a room, a simple room,
Perhaps a little bare,
But full of dreams and memories,
For family love is there.

# Friendship's Door

Hilda Butler Farr

How nice to knock on friendship's door,
And then to watch it open wide,
To see a smiling face, a hand
Outstretched to draw you close inside.

Within a cozy lamplit room
You find what riches cannot give,
A friend to whom you tell your dreams,
Whose faith has shown you how to live.

The sorrow that your heart has held
Is lightened while you linger there.
The world is very far away
As understanding fills the air.

Whatever life may hold for you,
And whether you are rich or poor,
You have the finest gift of all
If you knock on friendship's door.

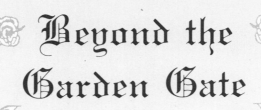

# Beyond the Garden Gate

Georgia B. Adams

The garden gate without a word
A welcome speaks;
Beyond its portal every flower
My friendship seeks!

And when I cross the threshold there,
What meet my eyes
But lacy-edged, gay faces filled
With glad surprise!

I pluck a nosegay, small and quaint,
From this array;
'Tis sure Nature would never miss
Them anyway!

And when I close the garden gate,
I leave behind
A friendship, that, when I return,
I'm sure to find!

# Thoughts
Hildur Solberg

Friendly thoughts
Are like fragrant flowers,
Filled with the perfume of love,
Binding themselves
Into one huge bouquet,
Blessings from Heaven above!

Friendly thoughts
Are like fragrant flowers,
Symbols of happiness,
Hiding the clouds
With sunshine so bright,
Hearts filled with thankfulness!

# Friendship Is a Flower
Sister M. Norbert F.D.C.

Friendship is a flower
In life's garden grown,
Thriving in the sunlight
Of each kindness shown.

Friendship is a flower.
Keep it free from weeds.
Never be distrustful,
Speak your love in deeds.

Friendship is a flower.
Nurture it with care.
Let your friends be mentioned
In your every prayer.

Friendship is a flower,
Scented, kissed by dew,
Catching in its chalice
Thoughtful acts from you.

Friendship is a flower
Redolent and pure;
Tended with affection
It will long endure.

Friendship is a flower
Placed in true heart's vase,
Bringing peace and comfort
All your days.

# June Sound

Florence A. Cass

The wind blows soft and scented.
   The summer homes spring alive.
There's low-pitched meadow music,
   And bees on the roses thrive.

     Sparrows sing in the golden green
       And the mating partridge drums
     The song of the brooks and birches
       As the silvery salmon comes.

The sound of summer vacations,
   Lawn mowing and cleaning of sheds,
There's graduating and lolling,
   And gardens reaching from their beds.

     Frogs peep in the rippling marshes.
       Deer drink in the dewy dawn.
     June-bugs splattering windshields,
       The dandelions fuzzy and long.

There are barbecues and camping,
   Beach parties and wee happy feet.
As midsummer beauty is nearing,
   Our golden June days, color sweet.

# June

June's banner in triumph is flung o'er the land
In all the rich loveliness at her command.
While perfume, of roses and lilies combined,
Joins in a service of tribute, we find.

Yes, deep-shaded forest and sun-flooded field
Are joining together, full homage to yield.
From bird on the wing to each blossoming flower,
Comes beauty and praise for each swift flying hour.

Elsie Campbell Grant

# Someone Special

Hilda Butler Farr

There's someone very special
I found along the way,
Who knows my deep affection,
The words I do not say.

How changed would be the story
Without this someone dear,
Who shares my hopes, my dreaming,
And laughs away a tear.

Companionship so priceless
And understanding, too,
Who is this someone special?
My daughter, it is you.

# A Mother's Concern for Her Daughter

Grace Mathews Walker

I am anxious, yes, my dear,
About your life and future happiness;
Yet I do not worry much
That your ideals fail
And drop you in the dust.

I've watched your loveliness
So sweet and pure,
As roses in the bud
By sunshine kissed,
Unstained by storm,
And blessed by heavenly dew.

A sense of joy
That makes for many friendships,
A self-respect
And value of the right—
These I see in you.

I'm sure that you possess
Rare courage and a daring
That will help you make
Decisions that are true,
And on them firmly stand,
Lest someone try to change
You from your better self.

I am most anxious, dear,
That life be kind to you,
But, more than all,
That you remain always
As lovely as you are today.

# The Ice-Cream Tycoon

Dr. Donald R. Stoltz

Ira Cohn sat gazing out of the window of the jumbo-jet airplane as it winged across the country from New York to Los Angeles, but his thoughts were not on the flight. He was thinking of his old friend, George Green, and the happy experiences they had together many years ago. Ira had not heard from George since they graduated from high school twenty-five years prior. That is, not until he received a strange letter in the mail with five airplane tickets for himself, his wife, and his three children.

He thought about the letter and the call that preceded it, from a woman, asking how many children he had. She informed him that Mr. George Green wanted his entire family to visit him as his guests. The letter simply read:

Ira,
If it wasn't for you, there wouldn't be me.
Now I want you all to come and see.
I made it big, 'cause I make it good,
And only you really knew I would.
George

Ira knew that George was a bit strange and the letter proved he hadn't changed, but his curiosity overwhelmed him and he was west coast bound.

As he gazed through the window at the beautiful, white fluffy clouds that looked like huge mounds of whipped cream, he turned to his wife and said, "Boy, old George really loved his whipped cream and did he love ice cream, any flavor, any shape, any time of the day or night. Popsicles, sundaes, cones, milkshakes, he really was an ice-cream addict. If only he loved school as much!"

"George was by far the poorest student in the high school class and if it wasn't for me, he'd probably still be there," Ira said. "Gosh, how many hours I would sit with him just to drill that math, English and history into his head." "Cohn, how can I thank you?" he'd say over and over again. Often he would call with his favorite little rhyme, "Hi, Cohn, Green on the phone and I need help with the homework." I remember so well before a test he would come running over to my house and scream, "Cohn, help me! It's driving me crazy!"

"But he was my friend and that's what friends are for," Ira thought. "Well, anyway, I got him through and the day we graduated I treated him to a big vanilla, chocolate, and strawberry sundae. He was more excited with that than with graduation." Ira smiled as he thought about it.

"Well, after that," Ira continued, "I went on to college and George moved away, and I never heard from him again until that letter. I wonder what he looks like? He must weigh three hundred pounds if he's still eating ice cream the way he did," he said. "I wonder what he's doing?"

Suddenly, Ira's thoughts were interrupted by the captain's announcement that the plane was landing, and soon the Cohn family was in the main terminal of the Los Angeles Airport. Ira stared at each face hoping to recognize George, but this was twenty-five years later and he was sure that he had changed.

"Cohn!" a voice suddenly boomed out. Ira spun around and was startled to see a handsome, gray-haired, suntanned, well-dressed gentleman walking briskly toward him with his hands outstretched. "Cohn, you old computer, you look great and this must be your family. Welcome to Los Angeles and thank you for coming."

"Thank you for inviting me, George, but I'm bursting with curiosity, why?"

"Well, just let's say I'm repaying a long overdue debt."

They talked about New York and reminisced about high school days as they walked through the terminal toward the exit. As the Cohn family and George walked out of the terminal, a huge limousine pulled up, a chauffeur got out, opened the door, and said, "Where to, Mr. Green?"

"To the house and then the factory, Henry, and call my wife. Tell her we're on our way."

The two friends spoke again of old times as they rode. Soon they entered, through a large, iron gate, a palatial estate. "Here we are!" George exclaimed, "just in time for lunch." The Cohn family gasped at the awesome size and beauty of the Green estate and Ira couldn't contain himself.

"My gosh, George! What? Where? When? How did you do it?"

"Patience, my friend, you'll find out."

Soon the Cohn family and the Green family were exchanging greetings, and hearing stories about boyhood adventures and the bygone days of the two men. After a lavish lunch, followed by an ice-cream dessert which made Ira smile and realize that George hadn't completely changed, the families said good-bye. The Cohns were guided back into the limousine.

"To the factory, Henry," George Green directed.

Ira was spellbound as the car sped along the highway and suddenly George pointed ahead and stated, "There it is!" Ira's eyes popped open wide as he gazed out the window toward a huge, industrial plant surrounded by high trees. As he looked upward, the color drained from his face. High on the roof of the building was a monstrous ice-cream sundae, with a great multicolored sign beneath it, which read, "COHN ICE CREAM."

"George, I don't understand," stuttered Ira, as his wife and children gazed in disbelief. "Why my name?"

"You'll see in a few minutes," smiled George, as they got out of the limousine and started to walk toward the factory entrance, along a magnificent path of trees, flowers and fountains.

"Ira," George began, (he never called him Ira before), "You have been the most important person in my life. You were a friend when I needed a friend, you helped me when I needed help, and you gave me confidence when I needed confidence.

When I arrived in California twenty-five years ago and decided to stay, I knew little and had nothing. I got a job selling ice cream and slowly learned the business. Everytime I had a problem which I couldn't solve, I'd stop and say to myself, 'What would Cohn do?' And each time I made the right decision with your help.

"Finally I bought a small ice-cream business, then a bigger business, then a factory, and today I am one of the largest ice-cream producers in the west."

"But why Cohn Ice Cream? Why my name?" Ira asked.

"Ah, there's the answer straight ahead," George said. Again the Cohn family stopped and stared in disbelief. There at the end of the walk, near the entrance to the factory, was a statue of Ira Cohn and under it read the inscription:

*"Ira Cohn — A Friend, An Advisor, An Inspiration, When I need an answer, I Scream Cohn!"*

# So Much Is Ours

Emily Selinger

So many things we wish for every day,
So ill content with blessings by the day,

But much is ours that's really worth the while:
A song, a prayer, a greeting and a smile,

A rift of sunshine in a stormy sky,
Health-giving winds of heaven passing by,

Sweet scent of roses, breath of forest wild,
Faith, hope and love, the laughter of a child.

And richer gift no grace of heaven can send
Than hearty handclasp of a faithful friend.

# My Prayer

Louise Gewin

Dear Lord, I pray for simple things:
A song, a smile,
The joy of friendship true,
Friendship that warms my very soul
And thrills me through and through,

A sparkling stream where sunlight's caught
And flashed at me again like rippling laughter,
A bird on high in the clear blue sky,
A violet hid neath a stone,
My baby's little pattering feet
And his precious smile are mine to greet,

A kitchen bright with dishes blue,
Someone's eyes that shine like morning dew.
I pray for these simple things,
Don't you?

# Letters

A few words drifting over time and space
Can bring a warmth, a glow of friendliness;
A voice unheard, a loved one's absent face
Return with written words. A soft caress,
The echo of an old forgotten song,
Between the lines, a sudden, clear reflection
To fill the heart with pleasure, deep and strong,
Brings back again a voice's dear inflection.
Across the miles, the handclasp of a friend
Reaches out within a letter's lines,
And down a little lane dream footsteps wend
Where memory's flowered tendril greenly twines.
From homefolks come small messages we love;
Just little things that bring a bit of cheer,
And, like sun smiling through the clouds above,
Are cherished words of someone we hold dear.
Oh, letters are like angels without wings
That come to us as if on magic flight,
Can evoke tears or happiness that sings,
Bright little flames that light the darkest night.

Ruth B. Field

# Pen Friends
## Language Knows No Barrier

My bare feet slapped the hard pavement as I jogged to the mailbox. Imperceptibly the radiant June sun began to slowly toast my already pink shoulders. Glancing into its brilliance, I thought, "Today I can believe this is the same sun that shines over Lucinda in Mexico." I smiled down at the letter in my hand and slowed to a walk, thinking about how it all began nearly nine years ago. . . .

Even before I sauntered into the classroom and plunked myself down into the seat farthest from the teacher and nearest the windows, I had decided Spanish 202 would be a terrific bore. Already a veteran of two junior high school Spanish classes, followed by one in high school that repeated everything learned in the first two, I was well acquainted with the routine and had no real desire to submerge myself into it again. In fact, the only basis for my present enrollment in the course was the advice of my counselor. He had, in no uncertain terms, stressed the importance of knowing a foreign language before entering college. Since I desperately wanted to attend an institution of higher education in the near future, I did not argue with someone whom I thought knew what he was talking about. Little did I realize what a profound effect the study of that particular language would have on me.

Not one to waste precious time on trivial introductory material, my Spanish teacher, Senora Ramirez, dove into work immediately by assigning several projects. One of these, not necessarily unique, yet new to my realm of experience, involved the selection of a name from a list of Mexican students who had agreed to participate in a cross-cultural pen-pal program. This particular project was designed to increase the student's ability to think and reason directly and automatically in another language, eventually eliminating the need for conscious translation.

Somewhat skeptical about the benefits of such an assignment and totally lacking in enthusiasm, I chose a name, Lucinda Maria Costanza Rodrigues da Hermosilla. I chose her name because it was the shortest one on the list! Poor Lucinda had no choice in the matter.

My first letter, written entirely in Spanish, consisted of little more than, "Hello. My name is . . . ," somewhat redundant considering I signed the letter with my full name. The second was no less innocuous. Lucinda's responses were, for the most part, English translations of my letters. I could not speak for Lucinda (that was obvious enough), but I knew I was suffering from a severe deficiency in conversational Spanish. By the time the third letter rolled around, I decided I had better find something interesting to write about before my pen pal wrote me off.

"But what," I reasoned, "would someone living in Mexico City be interested in hearing about? Perhaps more to the point, what would I be interested in writing about?" I had already covered such scintillating topics as the weather, the names, heights, weights and ages of my family members, and the kinds of food I preferred to eat. (Those vocabulary drills certainly came in handy.) After all that, what could possibly remain open for discussion? Since my mind kept drawing blanks, I started jotting down random thoughts, hoping eventually to break through my writer's block. If nothing else, I could at least practice writing in Spanish.

As I began writing, all my frustrations poured out on the paper until I found myself explaining in Spanish, a minor miracle in itself, how I had difficulty thinking of something to write to Lucinda, how I resented being forced to write to her for my class, how I considered the whole idea of pen pals worthless, and, eventually, how my little brother had caused me nothing but trouble all that day. Before I knew it, my purposeless ramblings had coalesced into a rather lively, though one-sided, discussion on the trials and tribulations of elder sisterhood. Occasionally I seized my Spanish dictionary to search for the badly-needed Spanish equivalents for *horrible, selfish* and *spoiled,* but for the most part I had no difficulty finding words to express myself. At the end of this rather lengthy tirade, I asked Lucinda whether she ever encountered the same problems with her two little brothers.

Amazed at what I had written, and even more amazed by the fact that it was all in Spanish, I decided to mail the letter immediately, before I could change my mind. "What can I lose," I thought, "but a somewhat dissatisfying relationship with my pen pal?"

One week later, I was shocked to read Lucinda's reply. Rather than finding my tactless note offensive, she readily identified with my sibling relationship and proceeded to elaborate on her relationships with her brothers. We had both discovered that sibling rivalry knew no bounds as far as nationality was concerned, and neither, for that matter, did friendship. Through those discoveries, we solved our problem of communication.

Once we had established a common bond, the strain was immediately lifted from our correspondence. Ideas flowed back and forth across the border unhampered by language or cultural bar-riers. Lucinda and I discerned far more shared interests than differences between us, and we launched a concentrated effort to explore every one through our letters. An unexpected benefit resulted from our mutual revelation—self-discovery. By setting myself down on paper for Lucinda to see, I could not help but learn a great deal about myself in the process.

From that point on, we corresponded faithfully at least once a month. Every year for birthdays, Christmas, graduations, and often for no particular reason at all, we exchanged a wide variety of unique gifts. One Christmas Lucinda sent me a delicate clay bell molded in the shape of a bird to hang on my tree. I sent her a miniature red velvet sleigh with Santa and his elves riding atop a mountain of angel's hair. On my twenty-first birthday, the mailman delivered a fringed shawl embroidered with every color of the spectrum. Last year, when I returned from my trip to New England, Lucinda received a tin of genuine maple syrup accompanied by a recipe for buttermilk pancakes.

The gift I treasured above all the others, however, was a copy of a simple, Mexican folk song, "El Corazon Alegre," which means "My Happy Heart." It was Lucinda's wedding gift to me. I wished she could have been present to hear it sung during the ceremony.

In view of our kindred spirit relationship, I had always found it ironic that we have never met face to face, never even exchanged photos of ourselves. The one opportunity I had to fly with my Spanish class to Mexico, I contracted a severe case of the flu and remained at home, bed-ridden. And yet, Lucinda and I were close, if not closer than sisters, and have remained so for the last nine years.

I was hoping to visit Mexico City sometime in the near future and looked forward to our meeting with eager anticipation. I had always been curious to see how closely we would fit our image of each other. . . .

The clang of the mailbox lid and my neighbor's "hello" roused me from my daydreams.

"So, another letter for Mexico," he commented. "When are you ever going to get around to seeing your pen pal?"

"Very soon, I hope," I replied. And with that I slipped my envelope into the box, bid my neighbor a good day, and jogged home singing "El Corazon Alegre."

Beverly Rae Charette

# ELEMENTARY, MY DEAR WATSON

Martin Tregoning

What a fortuitous meeting on that winter's day in London 100 years ago! Fortuitous not only for the two men who were introduced by a mutual acquaintance, but for the generations of readers and mystery fans since, who have made the accounts of what happened subsequently possibly the best known literary products in the world. For, on New Year's Day, 1881, Sherlock Holmes, a "private consulting detective" who plied his trade without much concern of financial gain, met John H. Watson, a severely wounded and pensioned army surgeon, who was having trouble of his own making ends meet during his recuperation.

A more agreeable match could hardly be imagined. The two complemented each other perfectly, and the nature of their relationship became evident from the moment of their meeting.

"You have been in Afghanistan, I perceive," said Holmes, who delighted in such startling statements.

And Watson, who was maybe twenty-eight at the time, two years older than Holmes, was suitably impressed, both with the physical appearance of his new friend and with his perspicacity. Holmes stood six feet tall, maybe a bit taller. But he was slim, and his erect bearing gave him an appearance of being even taller. His eyes were sharp and piercing and he had a hawk nose and a square jaw. He had an air of alertness and precision, characteristics that paid off in his profession.

Not that Watson was a buffoon. On the contrary, he was in some ways superior to Holmes. He was handsome, for example, with regular features, dark brown eyes, a moustache, and a kindly, warm demeanor that endeared him to women. Holmes, a confirmed bachelor, acknowledged Dr. Watson's advantage over him when it came to women.

At the time of their meeting, Watson was wasted away from his grievous wound in the Afghan War, poor, and friendless. Holmes' two-bedroom flat "with a single large airy sitting-room, cheerfully furnished and illuminated by two broad windows" at 221B Baker St. was just what he had been looking for—comfortable lodging and much less expensive than a hotel. Likewise, Holmes was friendless.

Still, they are cautious and confess their shortcomings to each other. Watson is brief and frank. He has a quick temper, he said, yet objects to arguments because of his nerves and tends to get up at all sorts of ungodly hours. "And I am extremely lazy," he said. "I have another set of vices when I'm well, but those are the principal ones at present."

For his part, Holmes was more circumspect, "I get in the dumps at times and don't open my mouth for days on end." He also smoked cigarettes and pipes with awful mixtures of tobacco (he was not above doing so intentionally to annoy). He was quiet in his ways and his habits were regular.

Holmes also admitted to playing the violin, but it is not so bad. He is a virtuoso.

Watson was the embodiment of all that it meant to be an English gentleman. He was stable, sober, honest, straightforward, courteous, brave. "If I have one quality upon earth, it's common sense," Watson noted.

And Holmes admired him for that, in his way.

"I have never loved," Holmes said himself. " Yet, I am lost without my Boswell," the detective confessed once. And again, when Watson was shot with a revolver, Holmes reached what may be his pinnacle of emotionalism, "You're not hurt, Watson? For God's sake, say that you are not hurt."

"It was worth many wounds," Watson confides, "to know the depth of loyalty and love which lay behind that cold mask."

This was true friendship, based on mutual respect and admiration. And Watson recognized his role, "I was a whetstone for his mind; I stimulated him. He liked to think aloud in my presence. If I irritated him by a certain methodical slowness in my mentality, that irritation served only to make his own flame-like intuition and impressions flash up the more vividly and swiftly."

"It may be that you are not yourself luminous," Holmes told Watson, "but you are a conductor of light. Some people, without possessing genius, have a remarkable power of stimulating it."

It was a relationship that transcended the desires of its creator, Doyle, who tried to end Holmes' career in a draw with his archenemy, Professor James Moriarty.

Despite the admonishment of even his mother, who wrote to Doyle, "You won't, you can't, you mustn't end the series prematurely," the two protagonists, in mortal combat, fell over Switzerland's Reichenbach Falls.

Public outrage was immediate. Twenty thousand readers cancelled their subscriptions to Strand Magazine, in which the stories appeared. Finally, Doyle revived Holmes after a three-year hiatus in the East. He appeared, messianically, to Watson, who fainted dead away. In all, Doyle wrote fifty-six short stories and four novels. From them have come 200 movies, uncounted radio and television plays, and Holmes societies (really more than fan clubs) that have taken such colorful and symbolic names as The Afghanistan Perceivers, The Baker Street Irregulars, The Speckled Band, and Dr. Watson's Neglected Patients.

Fifty-one years after Doyle's death and fifty-four years since the last Holmes-Watson story appeared, hundreds of letters are sent to Holmes each year, and a British savings and loan society that occupies the Baker St. address (which didn't exist a half-century ago) has an executive secretary who answers them. Perhaps no fiction character ever created has become so charmingly real to his readers.

It is a fitting and lasting tribute to the friendship of two men.

# The Flower of Friendship

Helen Steiner Rice

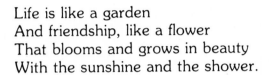

Life is like a garden
And friendship, like a flower
That blooms and grows in beauty
With the sunshine and the shower.

And lovely are the blossoms
That are tended with great care
By those who work unselfishly
To make the place more fair.

And, like the garden blossoms,
Friendship's flower grows more sweet
When watched and tended carefully
By those we know and meet.

And, like sunshine, adds new fragrance
And raindrops play their part,
Joy and sadness add new beauty
When there's friendship in the heart . . .

And, if the seed of friendship
Is planted deep and true
And watched with understanding,
Friendship's flower will bloom for you.

# Iris

Iris, you so fascinate, that through the night
I cannot wait
To see you touched by amber sun,
When at last the morn
Has just begun.

With ruffled skirts, you stand alone
'Long a wall of orchard stone
To dip and bow your lacy head,
As if to say, "Praise all my beauty,
Drink in the sight
Of dew-touched petals,
Of beards of white."

You stand in shades of softest blue, orchid, gold,
And lavender, too,
Proudly swaying in the breeze,
Bowing, nodding to the trees.

Rose Emily Houston

# Craig E. Sathoff

"I've loved poetry as long as I can remember and I'm sure I wrote my first poem in second grade," reflects Craig Sathoff. Since his childhood, he has enjoyed giving his poems to people, sometimes marking specific occasions.

Mr. Sathoff is a native and lifelong resident of Iowa. Growing up in the small town of Titonka created in him an inherent love of the small town way of life. He has succeeded two previous generations of school teachers in his family, having taught English and creative writing for the past twenty years in Iowa Falls.

Much of Craig Sathoff's writing reflects an appreciation of the past, as does his antiquing, an absorbing hobby. Other interests of his include cooking, gardening, and community theater work. He and his wife, Mary, enjoy their fine family, four sons and a daughter.

Teaching has been a most rewarding experience for Mr. Sathoff. Of his creative writing classes, he comments, "I am continually pleased to see many of my students become quite accomplished poets. There is a fellowship among poets that's hard to beat."

## The Way to Be a Friend

The way to be a friend is just
To strive each day to be
A firm believer in the strength
Of human dignity.

To teach each fellowman the way
That you would like to be,
With deep respect for each man's worth
And his integrity.

The way to be a friend is just
To keep a smiling face,
To realize that laughter adds
A special note of grace.

The way to be a friend is just
To give and give and give
Of help and care and kindly words
Each day that you shall live,

To shun away each petty doubt
And open up the heart,
To let in thoughts of love and trust,
Which is how friendships start.

## Quiet Things

A baby's gentle slumbering,
A dancing cloud above,
A friendly smile across the room
Are quiet things I love.

When friends are true they need not speak
Each minute they are near,
For quiet times when shared by friends
Are meaningful and dear.

An unborn infant's silent voice,
The calm of nesting doves,
A tear of joy, a handshake firm
Are quiet things I love.

A lazy snow that covers all,
A hand to guide the way
When footsteps falter in their goal,
All know the quiet way.

I thank my God for quiet things
Which come to bless my day
With gentle peace and harmony,
Each in its special way.

## A Loving Friendship

A loving friendship does not age,
It doesn't have the time,
For thought and care and helpfulness
Are always in their prime.

## Blue on Blue

There's beauty in a field of grain.
A rose is lovely, too,
But I reserve a special place
For things of blue on blue.

Blue skies reflected in the morn
Upon the river blue,
A baby's blue and sparkling eyes,
His blankets bluish, too.

A bluebird flying through a sky
Of deepest azure hue,
A note of love in deep-blue ink
On paper pastel blue.

Delphinium of varied shades,
A sky just after rain,
A ribbon on a lacy dress
Brings blue on blue again.

Blue brings a mood of gentleness
With shades of gentle hue.
I always feel a sense of ease
From soothing blue on blue.

## Walk a Summer Road

To walk a summer road is bliss,
To walk it calm and slow,
Beside the fields of golden oats—
What peace there is to know!

A summer road leads to the creek
Where stands the covered bridge
That casts its shade upon the spot
We used to fish as kids.

A summer road winds here and there.
It bends to fit your will,
Through waist-high corn,
Through bygone years,
Through lushly wooded hills.

There is a time for rest and hope
Upon a summer road,
To leisurely reflect the dream
Before you bear your load.

To walk a summer road is grand.
It saturates the heart
With strength and gentle harmony
That it so well imparts.

## You Took the Time

You took the time to stop and chat
As you passed by today,
To jest a bit in pure delight
Before you went your way.

You took the time to lend a hand
When I was faced with care,
To give the strength of fellowship,
To comfort and to share.

You took the time to send a note
On every special day:
A birthday card, a valentine,
A wish for Christmas Day.

You took the time for words of praise
That warmed me through and through.
You took the time to be a friend,
So patient, kind, and true.

# A Faithful Friend

He asks but little, just a kindly word,
A gentle pat can fill him with real bliss,
Or, humbly, just to lie close to your feet
And sometimes touch your hand with gentle kiss.

If you are feeling sad, he is sad, too,
And gives you sweet condolence with his eyes.
Your presence is the dearest thing he knows,
You are the sun that's shining in his skies.

A little dog so faithfully can be
Your truest friend, he really understands
Your every mood  and shows his boundless love
So eagerly obeying your commands.

Horizons go no farther than your face,
To him you are the stars and moon above.
He'll follow you to any distant place,
His eyes shine with a deep, unchanging love.

No matter who you are or what you do,
Your dog remains a true, devoted friend.
He'll share your life, though hungry, poor or cold,
And kiss your hand, quite faithful to the end.

Ruth B. Field

# Mary, Come Back

Colleen L. Reece

Golden sunlight filtered through the fir trees. Blue sky overhead framed puffy clouds. It was summer; but the hum of bees, the smell of flowers, the warm rain-washed air didn't mean much to the five-year-old girl sitting on the steps of the old house.

What good was summer? What good was all the outdoors to play in when there was no one to play with?

The little girl's bare toes dug into the dust. Her older brother had lots of friends in the area, boys his own age. She was too little to play with them. Mother, who used to play with her, was busy with a brand new baby brother. Father was working hoot-owl shift because of the hot weather. There was no one left for the little girl.

When school started in the fall she would be going—but now the empty summer stretched ahead, long, endless. They lived three miles out of town; the nearest neighbors were a quarter-mile away, but none of them had any little children. One hot tear slid down the little girl's nose. She brushed it away as her mother called.

"Would you like to take a big tub in the sunshine and fill it with water? You can put on an old slip and play in it."

In a moment the little girl's gloom was lifted. Eagerly she lugged the big tub to the middle of the yard. Bucket after bucket was pumped from the old-fashioned pump, hauled over and dumped in. It took a long time. It took an even longer time for the sun to warm the cold well water.

Rocking the baby, Mother smiled as she heard a trill of laughter. It was good to see her daughter playing. But a puzzled frown crossed her face a moment later. She heard voices.

"No, Mary, don't splash me! The water is too cold!" In another minute, "Now it's your turn. You get in the tub!" The mother looked out the window. Had visitors come? No, the long driveway leading in from the dusty gravel road was empty. Yet the voices prattled on.

"Oh, Mary, you're so funny!" Finally mother put the baby in his basket to sleep and went out.

"Who are you talking to, dear?"

The face of her little girl was radiant.

"To Mary, Mother! See?" She pointed to the tub, empty now except for what was left of the water. "Mary, don't throw water on Mother!"

There was no one there; or was there? It was a question the mother would ask herself over and over during that summer, the summer that had once stretched barren and lonely and was now filled with joy for her daughter. No longer did she cry when her older brother went off to play; she had found someone of her very own.

"Mary" became part of the family during those summer months. She sat at the table with them, she slept with the little girl, she even went on walks with the family when there was time to get away from all the work. Little by little she became accepted, and no one showed any surprise anymore when the little girl talked with her friend.

"Mary, you have to take off your shoes before you can get in bed.

"Mary, Mother is going to bake cookies today. We get to help, but we mustn't get flour on the floor.

"Mary, don't be noisy. The baby is sleeping."

In a hundred ways Mary learned her lessons, as did the little girl who loved her so devotedly. She learned responsibility. She learned to share. She learned love and consideration. Everything from meals to toys to the latest kitten were shared with Mary.

And then it was the end of August. September would soon be there, and with it school.

"We are going to get new dresses for school, Mary! Look!" the little girl held up yards and yards of bright cotton prints, ready for her mother's skilled needle.

"I like the pansy dress best, Mary likes the orange one." Carefully the dresses were finished and hung away. There wasn't so much time for playing now, but every day the little girl and Mary got ready for school. The little girl could already read, she loved books so well; so she herself began teaching Mary.

"A . . aaaa. B . . buh. C . . cuh." September came, the last weekend before school. Labor Day passed, and the next morning the little girl would get on the big yellow school bus with her older brother and enter a new world. She had hoped and dreamed of this day for weeks! But she came home to the dinner table that night with her dreams shattered.

"How was your first day of school?"

"I don't like school! I don't like my new teacher!" Mother and Father were shocked. She had had such high hopes!

"But why?"

A big tear slid off the end of the little girl's nose and fell onto her plate. "She made some children stand in the corner. She gave out papers and said there was a picture on the back. She said not to turn over the papers. Some of the children turned them over. They had to stand in the corner in front of everybody!"

"Were you one of them?" mother asked gently.

"Yes." The sobs were heartbreaking. It was total disgrace.

"Did Mary have to stand in the corner, too?"

A shake of the bowed head. "No."

In the weeks that followed Mary was mentioned less and less. Sometimes the mother and father would ask about her, and the little girl always had an answer . . . Mary and she both got good grades. Mary and she both helped the teacher. Mary and she both got their papers up on the board with A's on them. But by the end of the school year Mary was seldom mentioned anymore. Mother and Father talked it over privately, deciding Mary was gone. But the summer would be the test. Would Mary come back? Strangely enough, the warm days seemed a little empty without hearing their little girl call to her playmate!

Golden sunlight. Blue skies. White clouds. Dark green trees. Summer came again, and with it came Mary!

"Don't track in dust, Mary.

"Let me help you with your lessons, Mary.

"Help me with the sweeping, Mary." She stayed all summer; but again, as the little girl became involved in school, Mary drifted into the back-

ground. This time she would not return; the next summer a new family moved in just down the road; they had children of their own. Now the little girl's shouts were answered by others in hide-and-seek, tag, statues, all the games children play. And now that she was a little older, even her brother and his friends sometimes included her in their games.

"Where is Mary?" Mother asked once, holding her breath. But her daughter's eyes were clear and untroubled.

"She went away," the little girl said simply.

Mary was gone, but not her influence. Along with the little girl, she had learned everything from manners to kindness. She had won a place in the hearts of the entire family. She was gone . . . but she would not be forgotten.

Nearly forty years have passed since that summer when Mary came to join the family. The father is gone now, the mother has grandchildren. The little girl is grown. But over those years there has remained the memory of Mary. Who was she? Why did she come? Why did she go? Was she part of the little girl herself, or a creation of her imagination, or an angel sent in compassion to a lonely child? When the little girl who grew into a woman looks back and remembers, it is with a half-sweet sadness. Yet there are times when Mary seems very real, very close.

And if, when golden sunlight, blue skies, white clouds and dark green trees proclaim the arrival of summer, the little-girl-turned-woman should bend and whisper to a lonely flower, "Mary, come back . . ." then turn with a laugh for own foolishness, no one will ever know but me.

Little boys were made to tease
    The little girls on earth.
They're filled with love and mischief,
    With make-believe and mirth.
They try their moms and test their dads,
    Make teachers shake their heads.
But, oh, they look so innocent
    When tucked off in their beds.

# Little Boys
Viki Grasse

Little boys, and broken toys,
    A shoe without a lace,
Dirty socks, a key that locks
    A secret hiding place—
Little boys make lots of noise,
    You see them every place—
Appetites, impromptu fights
    That put them in disgrace.

Little boys were made to seek
    The hows, the whens and wheres,
To scare their parents half to death
    Accepting foolish dares.
They bring home pets and tell their moms
    Each one they *have* to keep.
But, oh, they look so innocent
    When they are fast asleep.

## A Chinese Folk Tale

Oi Ling led the three ducks along the road, past the cherry trees. Her eyes lingered on the bright pink blossoms.

When she came to the edge of Chung Ah's rice field she caught a glimpse, just a flash of black hair and glistening broad shoulders, but the knowledge that they belonged to Pak Leung made her heart beat like the wings of a hummingbird. She halted the ducks for a moment until her breath came back and the blush faded from her cheeks, and then she proceeded toward the plum orchard to do business with his father.

"I will give you two sacks of rice," Chung Ah said after ten minutes of negotiation, "one basket of plums, and some lichee nuts."

"These are very fine ducks," Oi Ling said quietly.

"And a basket—," Chung Ah waved a slender, but well-calloused, hand in the air, "very well, two baskets of cherries."

Oi Ling dipped her head and shoulders in a bow of acceptance. "Shall I take the ducks to your pen?"

"It looks as though that won't be necessary," Chung Ah's glance had shifted over her shoulder. "Here comes my son. He can save you the trouble."

A sudden shyness fell on Oi Ling. "I had better go," she mumbled, turning away. But Pak Leung, his chest rising and falling from his long run across the fields, blocked her way.

"Don't go," he said, taking her hands in his. "It is time we talked to my father." Oi Ling shot an apprehensive look at Chung Ah whose eyebrows drew together in puzzlement. "It is time we tell him," Pak Leung went on, "that we want his permission to marry."

"Marry?" Chung Ah said the word as though he had never heard it before and Oi Ling's fingers curled nervously in Pak Leung's. "It's just that you are both so young," he explained without their asking. He rubbed his jaw with his hand. "However, I will not say no." Oi Ling and Pak Leung smiled joyously. "I will not say yes either. I will let the Wise Man on the Mountaintop decide."

So it was arranged that the next day Oi Ling and Pak Leung would climb the mountain and ask the advice of Tung-fang So. Neither one of them could sleep that night. They confessed it to each other as they worked their way to the Wise Man in the growing heat of the morning sun.

They ran until they were breathless and then ran some more, and at last they saw the house that looked like a small temple, decorated with delicate carvings of animals with wings, hook-beaked birds standing in graceful bamboo forests, and a man contentedly riding a giant fish. Tung-fang So welcomed them and took them inside. He would not let them speak of their reason for coming until he had brewed them a cup of lotus tea. Then they sat on the floor, and, folding his arms, occasionally nodding his head so that his spindly gray beard brushed the front of his robe, he heard all that they had to tell.

"Before I can give you an answer," Tung-fang So said when they were finished, "I shall have to ask you to do something for me." He excused himself for a moment, went to a large lacquered bowl, and came back with two eggs.

"These are newly hatched from the nightingale," the Wise Man said as he put one in Oi Ling's hand. She cupped her palm around the delicate oval. It had almost no weight at all.

Tung-fang So gave the second egg to Pak Leung. "For one week," he told them, "these eggs are your children. You must carry them every place you go, as one must do with a small, helpless child. You will not have to feed them, nor dress them, but you will have to protect them and see that they do not get broken. In seven days' time, when you return them to me, I will give you my answer."

They went back down the mountain, carrying their eggs, laughing. It seemed so silly, being mother and father to a pair of eggs.

Pak Leung soon saw that taking care of an egg is no laughing matter. The first time he went out into the field to do his work he had to spend a half hour finding a safe resting place for his egg. He dare not lay it on the ground for the ox, or one of the other workers, might step on it. Even in the crotch of a tree it could be pounced on by a hungry animal. Finally he tied it to his waist with his shirt-belt but then he had to walk very slowly, plowing behind the ox like an old man with stiff joints, and it took him half again as long as it usually did.

Oi Ling was nearly afraid to close her eyes at night. There were so many sisters and brothers in her house, getting up and down, sleeping restlessly on their straw mats on the floor, and stretching their arms and legs in all directions. She dozed fitfully, her arms making a wall between the others and her egg.

Wednesday Oi Ling's mother asked her to go into the village and buy two fishes, an eel and a bit of octopus. She was also to buy a new cooking pot and a piece of blue cotton. Oi Ling and her egg set out

happily. She loved going into the village. She could see the fascinating wares of all the merchants, combs and flowers for the hair, "happy-day" robes embroidered with bats swooping over rolling ocean waves. She could watch the little boats of the fishermen and squish her bare feet into the soft, wet sand. And she could visit with her friend Wang Mu. Oi Ling had tied a canvas sack to her back and the egg, wrapped carefully in a scrap of silk, rested inside.

Oi Ling felt very happy. In a few days' time she would become a bride and move to Pak Leung's house. Her father would buy her a "happy-day" robe and maybe two silk chrysanthemums for her hair and a pair of embroidered slippers, and Pak Leung would look at her with love. Oi Ling found her legs getting tired before she'd even passed the kumquat tree and then remembered that she'd slept little the night before. She looked longingly at the shady patch of grass beneath the tree's branches but knew she mustn't stop to nap. She had to meet the fishermen when they docked to get the choice of their catch.

Once she bought the two fishes, the eel and the bit of octopus, Oi Ling had to remove the egg from the sack and carry it in her hand. Then the cooking pot and blue cloth occupied her other hand so that when she met Wang Mu she was pretty well laden down.

"See?" Wang Mu smiled up into the sky. "I'm flying a kite that Kwok made for me. He says when he sees it sailing over the rooftops he'll know I'm thinking of him."

"I love flying a kite," Oi Ling said.

"Yes, it's a great day for it. Lots of wind. You want to fly my kite for a while?"

Oi Ling was going to reach out and give Kwok's kite a try but the egg was in one hand, the cooking pot and cloth in the other. Even if she put the pot down she had to hold the cloth for it would get dirty and there would still be the egg. "I don't guess so." She gave her friend an apologetic smile. "I think I'd better be getting home."

She told herself a girl her age shouldn't be disappointed about not flying a kite. But Wang Mu, pink-cheeked and sparkly-eyed, seemed to be having a lot of fun. "A lot of fun," Oi Ling mumbled as she walked homeward, her head bent against the wind.

Pak Leung came over Thursday with a big basket of plums.

"How are you doing with your egg?" she asked.

"It almost got broken yesterday," Pak Leung spoke softly, not wanting the rest of Oi Ling's family to hear. "It rolled out of my shirt when I was taking the ox to the stream to drink. I think it's cracked."

Oi Ling sucked in her breath. "Let me see." He dug carefully into his carrying place, brought out the tiny egg, and put it in Oi Ling's hand. Gently she turned it over, examining its fragile shell. "No," she said with relief. "It's just a mark. See? I can rub it away with my fingertip."

"Oh! I was worried. It's not easy you know."

"Day after tomorrow we can take them back."

Early Saturday as the sun was just beginning to give color to the morning sky, Oi Ling waited patiently at the base of the mountain for Pak Leung. When he came neither of them said anything but, with slow, thoughtful movements and serious faces, they started to climb. Finally, when they had climbed so high that the houses below looked toy-like and the roads like snail trails, Pak Leung sighed.

"I do not think Tung-fang So was crazy after all."

"Neither do I," Oi Ling admitted.

"As a matter of fact, he has shown me that he truly deserves to be called wise."

The old man ushered them in as he did before and when their tea cups were empty he folded his arms. "You came for the answer to your question?"

"You have already answered our question," Pak Leung answered. "We have brought back the eggs." He rose and went across the room. He reached inside his shirt. The egg was very warm from being close to his body. With a look at Oi Ling, he laid it back in the lacquered bowl. Oi Ling's hand had been curled around her egg so long it hurt to open it. Her fingers straightened out stiffly. She took a deep breath and then put her egg-child in the bowl next to the other.

They thanked the Old Man, bid him goodbye, and started down the mountainside. The air was warm but a strong breeze had come up. Pak Leung swallowed a couple of times and cleared his throat.

"It's just that I'm not exactly ready yet to be a father—not the kind of a father I want my children to have."

Oi Ling gave a little nod. "I know. I, too, am not ready. It makes me feel regretful, but also free."

Pak Leung reached for her hand. "It does not mean I do not love you."

"What?" The breeze was hurling his words away before Oi Ling could make them out.

"I said, I love you," Pak Leung shouted.

"I know," Oi Ling shouted back. Her cheeks had pinkened and her eyes sparkled. Down below the village and the country people had awakened. Wang Mu's kite peeked over the rooftops. The fair would soon begin. Hand in hand, Pak Leung and Oi Ling ran back down the mountainside.

Gerry Maddren

# As I Pass By

The path I choose in my way of life
May be rough, and hills, steep and long.
But as I pass by, I hope that I
Will not miss the wild bird's song

Or fail to see the flowers that bloom
By the wayside, or know
The joy of watching the sunrise,
Or bask in the moon's soft glow.

And as I journey day by day,
I will count it loss if I
Forget to share the good I find
With my friends, as I pass by.

Hope W. Gibson

# The Wandering Wild Asparagus

Numerous foreign plants have been introduced into this country, some of which have naturalized, spreading across the landscape. Although many of these have become pests, a few have been very useful additions to our flora. Among these is the asparagus, *Asparagus officinalis*, a native plant of Europe, which was widely used as food for at least the past two thousand years.

References are made to asparagus in the writings of the Greeks, Latins, ancient Arabians, early Europeans and Renaissance herbalists. In *Krutch's Herbal* of 1560, the herbalist Mattiola states that the plant was very commonly found in European gardens and that there was little difference between it and the familiar wild species. Although the herbalists considered the asparagus a desirable, healthy food, they were much more interested in the plant as an all-purpose medicine. They noted that if the plant was cooked in wine, the resulting potion was good for insect bites, and if held in the mouth, the mixture relieved toothaches. The roots were considered good for jaundice, sciatica, pain in the kidneys and difficulty in urination. Such uses have long since been discontinued, but the vegetable has become an increasingly more valuable food item.

Over the years new varieties of asparagus have been developed, but the wild asparagus of Europe and the United States is essentially the same plant as our modern types. In the wild, conditions are not always favorable and may result in thinner and smaller number of stalks, but the delectable flavor is always there. Since it is one of the first green vegetables of spring, people constantly seek it along our highways, fencerows, and fields. The pleasure of this activity is well expressed in Euell Gibbon's well-known book, *Stalking the Wild Asparagus.*

If you are interested in harvesting wild asparagus, locate the plants in the previous season or find them by means of their old dried stems which usually remain well into the next spring. Plants are found in sunny areas where the soil is at least moderately rich and is well-drained, but never extremely dry. In May and June the shoots can be snapped or cut off at ground level, thereby preventing damage to roots and unseen sprouts. Avoid the very thin and the branching shoots. Stop cutting after the first week in July. The sprouts are most tender when only two to eight inches tall and are growing in moist, rich soil. Asparagus spears, which are not immediately used, can be kept in good condition by refrigeration or freezing.

The plant is attractive enough to be a garden decoration, and a few asparagus clumps can be added to any garden or yard. The edible asparagus is two to four feet tall, with narrow, erect stems, threadlike branches, and needle-shaped leaves forming a plumy, airy crown. The flowers are inconspicuous tiny, greenish yellow blooms, but the bright red berries complement the feathery foliage. The branches are sometimes cut during the summer for enhancing bouquets. Three other species of asparagus are often used in floral arrangements and as houseplants.

If you wish to develop some asparagus clumps, plant as soon as possible in early spring. Select a sunny or very lightly shaded area with good, porous soil that can be kept from becoming extremely dry. The soil should be neutral, and lime can be added as necessary. For each clump, dig a twelve-inch hole about twelve to eighteen inches wide. At the bottom of the hole loosen the soil and add compost or well-rooted manure or a balanced fertilizer (as 5-10-15 or 10-10-10). Use one or two-year-old plants, preferably the rust-resistant varieties, as Mary Washington and Waltham Washington. Older plants are almost impossible to dig out and transplant because of the brittle, spreading root systems. The transplants should not be allowed to dry before being placed underground. The roots should be firmly imbedded in the soil at the bottom of the hole with the root parts well spread out. They should be covered with about half the soil, and after the shoots come up, the remainder of the soil is gradually added. Asparagus roots need a deep layer of porous soil over them as protection. They prosper from a mulch of leaves, compost or well-rotted manure applied and maintained throughout the year. Fertilize the plants after harvest and also a month later.

Asparagus should not be harvested until three years old. For this reason most people prefer to start with roots instead of seed, even though seeds readily develop. Two-year-old clumps would seem to be the best choice, but the brittle roots are too often damaged when being dug and transported.

With the increasing cost and decreasing supply of fresh asparagus, "stalking the wild asparagus" will continue to be popular. Many people will find that the fringe benefits of this activity are as valuable as the food itself.

Harold W. Rock

# Asparagus with Rarebit Sauce

¼ c. butter
¼ c. flour
1 t. salt
⅓ t. white pepper
⅓ t. dry mustard
1 c. milk
1¼ c. shredded Cheddar cheese
2 lbs. fresh asparagus, cooked
 (approximately 32 stalks)
4 c. cooked rice
8 slices bacon, cooked crisp

Melt butter in large saucepan. Stir in flour, salt, pepper and dry mustard. Slowly add milk to flour and butter mixture. Cook over low heat, stirring constantly, until mixture thickens and is smooth.

Remove from heat and add cheese; stir until cheese melts. Arrange 3 to 4 stalks heated asparagus on ½ cup portion rice. Pour ¼ cup rarebit sauce over asparagus. Top with strip of bacon. Serves 8.

# Invitation

Come out with me and let us share
Summer that blossoms everywhere,
Offering us the loveliness
Of flowers in their gayest dress.
Rose and daisy, buttercup
Lift their petaled faces up
As we walk along and see
Butterfly and bird and bee.
Golden cowslips by the brook
Beckon us to stop and look.
Let us gaze at beauty here,
Summer vistas far and near.

Louise Darcy

# So Love I, the Quiet Ways

As a sailor loves the sea,
So love I, the gentle land
That only seeks to nourish me,
And gentler grows beneath my hand.

As a sailor loves the sea
With its challenge never won,
So love I, the golden gleam
Of harvest fields when day is done.

As a sailor loves the sea,
So love I, the quiet ways
Of fertile fields where sunshine lies,
And peace is part of summer days.

Mary Locke Johnston

# Among the Pines

There's a place I know of still,
And it waits for my return.
It's a little country piece of land
I love,
Set deep within a mountain's home.

I lived and grew there as a child,
Roamed the pine-filled land, so free.
Now I long to hear once more
The familiar songs it sings,
Walk upon the soft and silent
Needles of the pine,

When in the evening there comes a hush
That falls on everything,
And the air is sweet and fragrant-laced,
And the breezes blow so tenderly about
Among the scented pines,
Among the halls of God.

Where the grove trees rise so big and tall
The sun is hardly seen—
Only now and then it finds sweet refuge
Against the cool and lovely earth—
Among the scented pines,
The trailways of my youth.

Joann Howard Escue

# Daisy Field

June dons her meadow bridal gown
With yards of daisy lace;
And for a small girl, summer-free,
There is no lovelier place.
For June must have her flower girls
To fashion crowns of bloom
And wears long graceful daisy chains
To please her ardent groom.

Though hands work busily and fast
Among the swaying flowers,
Time sends a lark-winged telegram
That through the hastening hours
The eager bridegroom's on his way.
June, hearing it, grows shy;
Then, trailing daisies down the lane,
She goes to meet July.

Esther York Burkholder

Friendship is the fragrance I cannot touch,
But its blossom makes my heart a garden of delight.
June Masters Bacher

# I Bequeath ...

All of my fortune,
The wealth I possess,
Everyday things
That bring happiness,
Blessings and feelings,
Moments to spend,
(Although slightly worn)
I leave to my friend.

WITNESS:
TIME is a treasure,
Each moment to use
For pleasure, for others,
Whatever you choose.
Remember that life
Is minute by minute.
Use it with care;
Put quality in it.

Let BEAUTY bless you,
A gift of the eye,
Sunlight and starshine,
A patch of blue sky,
Small pets and babies,
Great oceans, clear streams,
Breathtaking mountains
To fashion your dreams.

May you have MUSIC
To sweeten your days,
Mozart and folk tunes,
Strong hymns of praise,
Measures for marching,
Drum, horn and string.
Love is the message
The world longs to sing.

See NATURE's splendor
With childlike surprise;
Quick lightning fingers
Can zip up the skies.
Watch by the brook where
The doe brings her fawn
To rest in the shade—
One sound and they're gone.

Take hold of MEMORY,
A source of delight.
Pleasures of childhood
Come into sight.
Familiar faces,
Scenes of the past,
Friendship and memories
Are treasures that last.

CODICIL ...
May GOD be your strength—
May heaven attend!
These are the treasures
I leave to my friend.

SIGNED ...
Alice Leedy Mason

# A Friend

Like a gently rippling river
    Flowing through the land,
Like the stillness of the shoreline
    Filled with golden sand,
As the beauty of the sunset
    Hues that softly blend,
Is the glorious understanding
    Of a trusted friend.

On the mountain, in the valley,
    Wealth or poverty,
Health or illness, fame, misfortune,
    Matters not, you see.
Whether far apart or near,
    Where'er our paths may wend,
Comes the wonderful assurance
    Of a trusted friend.

Hildur Solberg

# Together

Together,
A symbol of love,
To live never apart,
Unity of purpose,
A bond,
Heart within heart.
Together,
We will weave
The pattern of life,
A tapestry of beauty,
Colors harmonious.
No strife mars the texture,
Though there be sorrows
And perhaps tears.
Happiness with each other
Will crown the coming years.

Paula Nelson

# Happiness

You made the day brighter
For me, my friend,
Because of your cheery smile,
Because of the words you said to me
When you walked with me awhile.
So when the day is done, my friend,
I think of you the while,
Of the cheery things you said to me
And your warm and friendly smile.

Velta Myrle Allen

The sweet,
Delicate being of you
Becomes the poem.
Words suspended
As though caught in flight
Remain captive.

They cannot soar
Into this golden
Realm of love.
Many gifts have I,
None so exquisite
As your gem of friendship
Generously given.
It is treasure
In my heart
Forever . . .
Mary Frances Watkins

# Sunset Over the Lake

A sunset over a clear blue lake
Is beautiful to behold,
Glowing, resplendent and picturesque
In crimson, purple and gold.
The golden stroke of the Master's hand
Adorns the western skies
In a picture that would warm the soul
Of all who would lift their eyes,

Giving warmth and cheer to the twilight,
Reaching to depths untold,
Casting a glow on the waters,
Turning the blue into gold.
Then it slips behind the horizon
And the afterglow fades into night,
And I know my eyes shall never behold
A more glorious and radiant sight.

Jean L. Roush

### ACKNOWLEDGMENTS

IRIS by Rose Emily Houston. From ROSES AND REMEM-
BRANCE, Copyright 1978 by Rose Emily Houston. MARY
COME BACK . . . by Colleen L. Reece. Originally published in
THE RURALITE, September 1980. THE FLOWER OF FRIEND-
SHIP by Helen Steiner Rice. Used with permission of the
author. ELUSIVE BUTTERFLY by Edna Moore Schultz. From
THOUGHTS ALONG THE WAY, Copyright 1980 by Edna
Moore Schultz. Our sincere thanks to the following authors
whose addresses we were unable to locate: Margaret E. Bruner
for THE FOOTBRIDGE from ETERNAL QUEST, Copyright
1968 by Margaret E. Bruner; Louise Gewin for MY PRAYER;
Mrs. R. Armistead Grady for TREASURE by R. Armistead
Grady; Paula Nelson for TOGETHER; Emily Selinger for SO
MUCH IS OURS which was previously published in SUN-
SHINE MAGAZINE, November 1951.

### COLOR ART AND PHOTO CREDITS
(in order of appearance)

Front and back cover, H. Armstrong Roberts; inside front and
back cover, Freelance Photographers Guild; Birdhouse, Fred
Sieb; Rustic bridge, Fred Sieb; Happy family, Freelance Pho-
tographers Guild; Hands of friendship, Robert Cushman
Hayes; Butterfly, Freelance Photographers Guild; Homespun
corner, H. Armstrong Roberts; Flowering trellis, Fred Sieb;
Colorful walkway, Freelance Photographers Guild; Flower
basket, Colour Library International (USA) Limited; Tiger
lilies, Freelance Photographers Guild; PORTRAIT OF MME.
VIGEE-LEBRUN AND HER DAUGHTER, Vigee-LeBrun,
Three Lions, Inc.; HOME FROM SCHOOL, Norman Rockwell;
Friendship thoughts, Fred Sieb; The sitting room, Gerald
Koser; Iris, H. Armstrong Roberts; Friendly nudge, Freelance
Photographers Guild; A helping hand, Camerique; Hollyhocks
along the lane, East Hebron, New Hampshire, Eric Sanford;
Flowers for you, H. Armstrong Roberts; Wheatfield, H. Arm-
strong Roberts; Horses grazing in scenic Wyoming, H. Arm-
strong Roberts; Columbine, H. Armstrong Roberts; Mt. Grin-
nell, Grinnell Lake, Glacier National Park, Montana, Ed
Cooper; Beaver Ponds, Rocky Mountain National Park, Colour
Library International (USA) Limited; Sunset on the lake,
Freelance Photographers Guild.

## A Salute to our Heritage . . .

Our next issue, Americana Ideals, proudly portrays the rich, varied resources that make our country great: our land, spirit, ingenuity, principles and people. Splendid color photography and artwork accompany an outstanding selection of prose, poetry and informative articles.

"Laura Ingalls Wilder: Stories That Had to Be Told" traces the life of a favorite American author. Walt Whitman, our best-loved poet, celebrates nature, freedom and the American people in his writings. Family picnics, fishing, strawberry festivals and other special, traditional summertime activities are featured in Americana Ideals.

Share all of these memorable moments by giving a special friend or relative a gift subscription to Ideals. Or subscribe for yourself and enjoy Ideals all year long!